GROWING UP SANE
(in uncertain times)

ISBN: 0-9648972-2-9

Acknowledgments

Many thanks to all of the people who contributed to the development and publication of this book. Most importantly, thanks to the young people who taught me to understand the importance of positive emotional development. Special thanks to my nieces, Casey and Sydney, who make the printed words come to life, and my pets, Chelsea and Kelley, who taught me the true meaning of flexibility and commitment.

TABLE OF CONTENTS

Table of Contents

Preface

About the Author

PREFACE

This book was written in response to the writer's frustration with the limitations of the current system being used for treatment of youth with emotional and behavioral problems. The pages that follow include some of the most important things, in the opinion of the author, that parents and caregivers can do to prevent many of the problems youth face today.

The set of skills and concepts in this book are referred to differently by various disciplines within the helping professions. For the purposes of this book the term positive emotional development will be used to summarize a broader array of traits that make us who we are. Those traits include: self esteem, self concept, self image, etc.

The recommendations are written in easy to understand and apply statements. However, do not allow the simplicity of the suggestions prevent you from grasping the depth of their meanings. Each is written based on psychological principles that are appropriate for children and youth in different stages of their young lives.

The underlying tenets are similar to Native American child rearing philosophy. If you are interested in more information regarding Native American customs and practices you may want to get a copy of the book "Reclaiming Youth At Risk: Our Hope for the Future" which is published by the National Educational Service.

Growing Up Sane (in uncertain times) is the first in a series of books about developing positive emotional development. The author hopes this information will increase your understanding of the emotional needs of children and youth of different ages, and enhance your skills and abilities as caregivers. Enjoy.

ABOUT THE AUTHOR

LuAnn Pierce, MSW is a social worker and youth counselor. At this time Ms. Pierce is pursuing her writing and publishing career under the umbrella of Bohemian Publications. A late bloomer who began college at age twenty-eight, she describes herself as having many interests that went unrecognized until she entered the world of higher education. She graduated form the University of South Carolina with a BA in Interdisciplinary Studies and a MS degree in Social Work. Ms. Pierce was honored by the faculty of the College of Social Work at USC in 1994 as one of two students to receive the coveted Outstanding Academic and Practice Achievement Award.

Ms. Pierce was raised in a small town in rural West Tennessee. A child of the seventies, Pierce admits the popular influences of the times were instrumental in molding her outlook on life. She describes herself as a person who is self aware, always evolving and seldom hesitant to amend her perspectives to reflect deeper levels of knowledge and understanding. She prides herself on her ability to relate to people and maintain a sense of "realness" with clients, readers and people in general.

Section I

Birth to Two Years; These Days Can Make or Break a Child

Attachment

to an adult that I can depend on for my basic needs is the most important thing in my life now.

(I 'm pretty helpless, but bonding with someone who loves me makes me feel more secure!)

*B*e very careful

with me, I am
physically and
emotionally fragile.

(I know . . . you are,
too - I will try to keep
that in mind!)

*C*uddle with me, it makes me feel safe.

(Admit it, you like it, too!)

*D*o things with me

'cuz I love your
company.

(I like to get out and
about, too.)

*E*xplore the world

from my eyes and you
can see how scary it is
for me ...

(after all, I am pretty
small.)

*F*orgive me if I

interrupt your routine
... I am not big enough
to care for myself yet.

(Someday you will
welcome the chance
to hear me ask for help
... hard to believe now,
huh?)

7

*G*rant me special,

private time with you,
today and forever, so
we can stay close.

(My spouse will just
have to learn to live
with it!)

H elp me by

teaching me to help
myself as I get bigger.

(But not too much, too
soon ... I _am_ still a
baby, you know!)

*I*ndependence is

the goal of youth ...
it begins at birth.

(and the quest really
never ends!)

10

*J*ust hold me the first
few weeks, I have
never been away from
my mommy.

(But, I will be, before
you realize it!)

Keep a close eye
on me as I begin to
crawl around...but
allow me to check out
the world around me.

(As long as there is not
a big drop-off on the
other side.)

*L*earn new things so
you can teach them
to me.

(Better hurry before
I think I know
everything.)

Moving around from home to home is very scary and I need as much stability as possible.

(Life's hard enough when you are totally dependent on others!)

New people and

places take a while for
me to adjust to ...
give me the time I
need to get used to
them.

(And keep me away
from the ones you
don't want me to be
like later in life!)

15

*O*ften it seems as
if there is nobody else
in the whole world but
you and me.

(Too bad we can't
keep it that way.)

*P*arents are life's

greatest gifts in the
eyes of a child.

(Don't make me regret
saying that.)

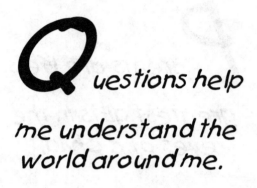

Questions help me understand the world around me.

(If someone only knew the answers!)

Read to me, please,
the sound of your voice
is soothing.

(P.S. -I love the
stories, too.)

Spending time with
me now may prevent
some of life's problems
later.

(You know, like me
coming back to live
with you when I am 35!)

*T*alking to me in a quiet voice makes me feel calm.

(And I am sure you want me to remain calm, don't you?)

*U*sing big words

confuses me
sometimes, so explain
them to me . . .

(in little words, please.)

Very loud noises

frighten me, so I may
need you to protect
me from them and help
me feel safe again
after that happens.

(It would be nice if we
could prevent that as
much as possible...
you know, by not yelling
or slamming doors?)

Walking for the first time is very exciting and a little scary.

(Hang on, here we go!)

X on the wall

means "I love you" in child language.

(See?)

Y early check ups
are a bummer ... unless
you help me
understand why it is
necessary to get them.

(Especially the shots.)

*Z*ebras are sort of
like children, beautiful
but hard to figure out
at first...

(Aren't we?)

Section 2

Two to Five Years: This Could Be the Last Chance for the Big People to Be in Control

ALLOW ME THE

FREEDOM TO TRY NEW
THINGS . . . *I* CAN DO IT!

(JUST WATCH THIS!)

*B*ELIEVE IN ME AS I

ATTEMPT TO DO NEW
THINGS . . . SO I WILL
BELIEVE IN MYSELF.

(YOU DON'T WANT ME TO
BE A FAILURE, DO YOU?)

Consistency is very important to help me learn what is right and wrong.

(I get confused when one person says it's okay to do something, and another says it is not.)

DISCIPLINE IS TO

TEACH ME WHAT IS RIGHT,
NOT TO PUNISH ME FOR
DOING THINGS THAT ARE
WRONG.

(NOW . . . WHY WAS I IN
TIME OUT THIS MORNING?)

EVERY CHILD STARTS
TO SLOWLY BECOME MORE
INDEPENDENT AS A
TODDLER.

(SEE, IT IS NORMAL - EVEN
THIS BOOK SAYS SO!)

*F*INDING OUT WHO I AM

IS A BIG JOB THAT BEGINS
NOW AND TAKES A
LIFETIME.

(WHO ARE YOU TODAY?)

GIVE ME

OPPORTUNITIES AND
CHALLENGES TO HELP ME
GROW.

(ESPECIALLY TO GROW
TALLER SO I CAN PLAY
BASKETBALL WITH THE BIG
KIDS.)

HAVING YOU THERE

FOR ME EVEN WHEN I
DON'T SUCCEED MAKES IT
EASIER FOR ME TO TAKE
CHANCES.

(IF YOU ONLY KNEW WHAT
I TRY WHEN YOU ARE NOT
AROUND . . .)

Inspire me to try new things.

(I don't want to miss out on anything.)

*J*UST BECAUSE I
MAKE MISTAKES DOESN'T
MEAN I AM DUMB, ONLY
HUMAN.

(I GUESS THE SAME GOES
FOR YOU, HUH?)

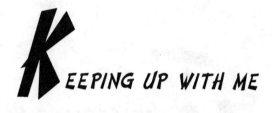

KEEPING UP WITH ME

MAY BE GETTING HARDER
EVERY DAY, BUT DON'T
GIVE UP . . . I STILL NEED
YOU CLOSE BY.

(JUST DON'T STAY TOO
CLOSE BY WHEN MY
FRIENDS ARE WATCHING!)

*L*IMITS HAVE TO BE
SET FOR CHILDREN TO
TEACH US HOW TO LIVE A
BALANCED LIFE.

(IN ALL AREAS OF LIFE?
EVEN WATCHING
TELEVISION?)

MOTHERS AND
FATHERS CAN BE KIDS'
BEST FRIENDS, AS LONG AS
THEY KNOW WHERE AND
WHEN TO DRAW THE LINE.

(AND THAT IS NOT
NECESSARILY WHEN WE ARE
AT THE MALL!)

Nobody likes to be
ignored when they have a physical or emotional need.

(Who came up with that one, anyway?)

OLDER PEOPLE KNOW

LOTS OF GOOD STUFF THAT
I CAN LEARN FROM THEM.

(IF THEY COULD JUST
MAKE THEIR POINT A
LITTLE FASTER!)

PEOPLE MAY

DISAPPOINT YOU IF YOU
EXPECT TOO MUCH FROM
THEM.

(. . . EVEN YOUR
CHILDREN — OR PARENTS
FOR THAT MATTER.)

QUESTIONS ARE ONE WAY ADULTS GET KIDS TO TALK MORE ABOUT THEMSELVES, THEIR THOUGHTS AND FEELINGS.

(BUT PLEASE, DON'T OVER DO IT!)

REMEMBER OUR

SPECIAL TIMES TOGETHER
SO YOU CAN REMIND ME
WHEN I AM OLDER.

(I HAVE A LOT ON MY
MIND, YOU KNOW.)

SPENDING TIME WITH

YOU IS NOT SOMETHING I
WILL OUTGROW, BUT THE
AMOUNT OF TIME WE SPEND
TOGETHER WILL CHANGE.

(YOU CAN'T GO TO SCHOOL
WITH ME, YOU KNOW!)

TELLING KIDS WHEN

CHANGES ARE ABOUT TO
TAKE PLACE GIVES THEM
TIME TO PREPARE FOR AND
ADJUST TO THE
TRANSITION.

(AND THINGS GO A LOT
MORE SMOOTHLY!)

*U*SEFUL INFORMATION

YOU CAN SHARE WITH ME
ABOUT NEW EXPERIENCES
MAKE THEM LESS FEARFUL
FOR ME.

(AND LESS CHAOTIC FOR
YOU.)

VASES THAT BREAK

CAN BE REPLACED,
CHILDREN CAN'T.

(NOW, ABOUT THAT
FLOWER ARRANGEMENT
ON THE DINING ROOM
TABLE . . .)

WHEN I ACT OUT IT
MAY MEAN THAT I NEED
SOME ATTENTION, NOT TO
BE IGNORED.

(DOCTORS DON'T KNOW
EVERYTHING, YOU KNOW.)

RAY VISION IS NOT
NECESSARY TO SEE WHEN
A KID NEEDS A HUG . . .
IF YOU SIMPLY PAY
ATTENTION TO US YOU
WILL KNOW.

(NOT TOO MUCH
ATTENTION, THOUGH!)

YOUR ACCEPTANCE IS

WHAT ALLOWS ME TO MAKE
MISTAKES AND KEEP
TRYING,

(AND TRYING, AND TRYING
AND . . .)

ZILLIONS OF KIDS

EVERY DAY HAVE THE
SAME NEEDS AS ME.

(. . . SEE, WE MAY ALL BE
DIFFERENT, BUT WE ARE
ALSO A LOT ALIKE.)

Section 3

Six to Nine Years: Enjoy it While You Can . . . It Won't Last

Asking questions

is one way I master new things in my world.

(The other ways are mysteries . . .)

Belonging to a group . . . like a family, club, church or class, is important for all kids.

(Maybe karate class? Or ballet?)

Communicate

your unconditional love and acceptance to me every day, in every way.

(Except in front of my friends.)

Doing things together as a family keeps us close.

(Can I go outside and play with my friends, now?)

Expose me to new

*ideas and different
ways of doing things
so I can learn about
life . . .*

*(life outside of our
home, that is!)*

Frightened

children need
someone they can
trust to talk with.

(Just like grown-ups
do when they are
afraid.)

*G*ive me

*responsibilities that
are right for my age.*

*(How about feeding
the cat?   Oh yeah,
can we get a cat?)*

*H*ear what I

<u>don't</u> say out loud
. . . actions and
expressions tell all!

(I learned that from
watching you.)

*I*nstruct me

without making me
feel foolish or
worthless.

(I'm still learning,
you know.)

*J*ust because I spend more time away from you now than in the past doesn't mean that I need you any less.

(I just need my friends more right now . . . you know, to learn how to get along with others, and all that stuff.)

*K*nowing the
importance of
structure and
keeping a regular
schedule teaches me
very important skills
for later in life.

(Are you sure about
that? This one may
need some more
research.)

*L*earn from me, I
have a lot to share.

(. . . except my free
time.)

*M*odel the behaviors you want me to use.

(And don't forget ... I am always watching!)

Now I am

*beginning to think
about things that
are important in life*

*(. . . this may be your
last chance for input
before I know
everything!)*

Opportunities to help other people at an early age teach kids like me compassion and empathy.

(Isn't that when you wear someone's shoes, or borrow their moccasins, or _something_ like that?)

Punishment

*needs to fit the
misdeed and teach
new behavior.*

*(I am still just a kid,
you know.)*

*Queens and
kings deserve no
better treatment
than I.*

*(I will remind you of
this if you forget.)*

Remove the words "never, ever, should, can't and won't" from your vocabulary . . . one can hardly live in the black and white areas these days.

(Especially when you have children.)

Sharing my

*things with others
may not come easily
for me, but I hear it
can be very helpful
in preparing for
adulthood.*

(Is that true?)

*T*ell me the truth,

even if it means
saying "I don't
know."

(Or saying "That is
nothing for you to
concern yourself
with!")

*U*se your

judgement to set limits that protect me, but teach me to think for myself and make informed choices.

(You will be glad you did, I promise!)

*V*iolence, even

when not directed
toward me, can be
very scary and leave
emotional scars . . .
at any age.

(Let's give peace a
chance . . . huh?)

Wellness as a lifestyle helps prevent many social and emotional ills, as well as physical ones.

(Is __that__ why we go for a walk together every evening?)

X out old beliefs

about how "things should be" that are not realistic for us in today's world.

(In case you haven't noticed, times have changed!)

Your dreams for

me may not be the
same as my dreams
for myself . . . but I
know you mean well.

(Sorry you never got
to fill-in-the-blank.)

Zooming in to

save me from the
consequences of my
behavior may cause
more harm than
good.

(I am not sure I
believe that one.)

Section 4

Ten to Twelve Years: Whose Kid is This, Anyway?

*A*dults mean well most of

the time, but sometimes I wish
they wouldn't help so much.

(Remember, helping too much
can be harmful!)

*B*elieve in me . . . I can

become anything you think I
can.

(As long as it's something I
want, too!)

Choosing friends is not an

exact science, so you may need to give me some help at times.

(Only on a rare occasion, I would imagine.)

*D*eveloping a positive

outlook on life can be contagious
. . . I may get it!

(And I have a feeling we may
need it over the next few
years!)

*E*xplaining my thoughts

and feelings is easier if I don't
have to defend them.

(Try to remember that I am a
separate person from you and
my thoughts and feelings are
my own.)

*F*orgive yourself when you

bomb out, not even parents are
expected to be perfect.

(See, I remember that one from
years ago. That goes for kids,
too!)

*G*ive me something special

to remember every day, even if
it is only a smile.

(And a hug if I'm in the mood
. . . and nobody is watching.)

Helping others may not

come naturally for me, but I can learn to give to others.

(I wouldn't want to go overboard . . . unless we could negotiate more free time for worthy causes!)

*I*nvolving people I trust in

decision making requires that
all of us remain open to the
possibilities.

(We may not even agree on the
choices, much less the merits of
each one!)

*J*udging me makes me feel

the same way you feel when
others judge you.

(*Did you get that?*)

*K*eeping your promises

builds my trust and respect
for you.

(I know . . . that goes
both ways!)

Learning about people who

*are different from me helps
prevent prejudice.*

*(Maybe I can help others learn
to tolerate differences
. . . and win the Nobel
Prize!)*

*M*ean people stink . . .

especially if they are your
parents.

("Meanness" is recycled over
and over . . . think about it!)

*N*ow and then things

happen that really upset me,
but may seem insignificant to
you.

(Be patient with me, my
feelings seem to be a lot bigger
than I am at times!)

Owning up to my mistakes

is a sign of maturity.

(I learned that one from you!)

*P*leasing others has a price

. . . you may resent them if you are really doing it to meet your own needs.

(Let's think more about that one. That is not the same as cleaning my room so I can go out, is it?)

*Q*uestioning young people

may result in a defensive response unless you choose your words and tone carefully.

(Ever noticed how that happens when someone questions you?)

Reaching a balance in life

helps people avoid excesses.

*(Does that mean work and
money, too?)*

*S*peak to me as you like to

be spoken to.

*(I'll try to do the same for you
and other people, too.)*

*T*easing is often a sneaky

way to say things that are
hurtful to others.

(Show me how to be assertive
so I can express myself without
hurting anyone.)

Use your natural talents

to help me discover my creativity.

(I need a creative outlet . . . even if it is in the form of the clothing I choose to wear, or my hairstyle!)

*V*enting your feelings is a

good way to keep your sanity,
as long as nobody gets hurt.

(At times like that I may just
need some space to work things
out on my own.)

Whining is an annoying

way to express your needs, as a child, youth or adult.

(Don't let me get away with that . . . I don't want to be shunned by everyone I meet!)

X marks in citizenship

on my report cards may
indicate difficulty coping with
the changes going on in my life
. . . better keep an eye out for
other indicators.

(Okay, so I may need some
help getting through
adolescence!)

*Y*elling at me usually

provokes me to react in the same manner, as does talking calmly.

(Want to try it both ways and choose your favorite?)

*Z*ipping through life

without a worry in the world is
every child's right, but
unfortunately it may not always
be possible.

(Try to find another grown-up
to share your problems with
. . . I am not the right person
to take on that role.)

Section 5

Thirteen and Forever: But . . . You're Still My Child

As annoying as it may be at times, I am just me, and I like to be accepted for who I am.

(Sorry I am not just like you . . . but being me is really not that bad!)

Being involved with

other people helps me learn more about who I am and who I want to be.

(I have been learning about you my whole life . . . I think I've got it, now.)

Coming of age is scary and exciting . . . I am never sure how I will feel from moment to moment.

(But I like the challenge of figuring it out!)

Deviating from the
norm may be a sign of a
talented or gifted person, or
one who chooses creative ways
to express his or her
uniqueness.

(Let me find out about
myself now - so I don't put it
off until middle age when I
need to be doing other
things! You know, working
and contributing to society.)

Evaluating my success

by the same ruler you
measure the success of others
may set me up for failure.

(As long as I am doing my
best, that's what counts,
right?)

Feelings are neither good nor bad . . . they simply are.

(There is no right or wrong way to feel about things . . . granted you may need to investigate if certain situations send me into orbit.)

Generosity has no strings attached, rather, a gift given in a spirit of generosity is freely offered with no expectations.

(H-m-m-m, how is that different from, "After all the things I do for you...?")

Hopelessness may be

a sign of deeper problems
that need to be
explored . . .

(I hear most teens have some
ups and downs, but they are
short lived and temporary.
Parents or caregivers should
pay attention to any
variations to that rule of
thumb.)

*I*nterests come and go -

ours may not always be the
same.

(Yes, I am growing up . . .
and I have interests of my
own, but I'm sure we still
have some common ground!)

Justifying my beliefs

and values makes me feel
unaccepted.

(Remember, my beliefs may
change from day to day for
the next few years . . . I am
learning a lot of new things
that need to be considered.)

Keeping a balance between home, school and friends takes practice.

(So-o-o, you may have to help me, at first, just a little.)

Laughing is good for the soul . . . remind me to love life and not take myself too seriously.

(Life is too short to be miserable.)

Making a choice to put off major decisions until later _is_ making a choice.

(Sure, the chance of a lifetime may slip away . . . but I have the rest of my life to do x, y, and z, _and timing is everything!_)

ot all teens fit the cookie cutter mold - attempts to force me to fit in can be damaging to my sense of well being.

(Peer pressure is hard enough to cope with - please don't do the same thing to me at home.)

Odd behavior may indicate that I am checking out who I want to be, not testing your patience.

(Let's face it, forming your identity requires exploring what's available.)

Privacy is important

for teens, please respect
mine.

(Even if you are just dying
to know what's going on -
unless I give you a reason to
question my safety.)

uandaries come
and go . . . with each one I
get more confident in my
ability to overcome life's
obstacles.

(Boy, do I ever get a lot of
practice!)

eaching goals

requires commitment and
sacrifice on my part, as well
as support and
encouragement on your part.

(Now, if we could only
agree on the goals.)

Speeches and lectures seldom get the same results as teaching and setting limits.

(Please don't go that route . . . trust me on this one!)

*T*alking it out can

prevent acting it out later
. . . let's make time to talk
about things.

(Just remember, if what's
bugging me isn't about you -
you can't change it.)

Unique describes all people, of all ages … . not just those who are visibly different from mainstream society.

(Did you get that?
Are you sure?)

Values are molded

early in life, but may be
refined and even challenged
during the teens and
twenties.

(It's not unheard of to share
differing views on issues than
those of your parents . . . we
may just have to agree to
disagree at times.)

135

Wonder keeps me

thinking and leads me to
explore the unknown.

(As in "Wonder if I can get
by with that?")

 - as in

Generation X, simply describes a group of people with similar characteristics or circumstances, not all of whom are apathetic and rebellious.

(Xers are simply the products of the Boomers, most of whom were children of the 60s and 70s, remember them?)

Yuppies, Hippies, Baby-Boomers and Dead Heads are also groups with similarities and differences.

(Ring any bells? Just another stereotype!)

Zany tricks and exploits are to be expected from youths, as long as nobody gets hurt.

(Physically or emotionally . . . I remember this one, too.)

INDEX

Service Directory

This section contains the names and contacts of groups who offer services and information that may be of interest to the reader.

American Self Help Clearinghouse
1-201-625-7101
Directory of over 500 support groups

Child Care Information Center
1-804-722-4495
Guidelines for choosing a child care provider for your child.

Parents Anonymous
1-800-371-3501
Listing of support groups for parents

National Clearinghouse on Family Support and
Children's Mental Health Services
1-800-628-1696
Information and referral services

National Council on Child Abuse and Family Violence
1-800-222-2000
Information and referral service

National Center for Youth with Disabilities
1-800-333-6293
Information and referral service

Visible Ink Press
Resourceful Woman Handbook
1-800-776-6265
Directory of over 800 pages of resources for women

Institute for Responsible Fatherhood and Family
Revitalization
1-202-789-6376
National project to improve the lives of children and
families through responsible fatherhood

Affinity Books & More
1-888-804-0826 PIN 8397
www.affinitybooks.com
On-line promotion and distribution of books, gifts and
services that promote emotional wellness. Specialize in
books written by professionals and self published books
that relate to the helping field. An on-line counseling
center offers counsel, consultation and referral from Ms.
Pierce and other professional helpers, as well as peer
helpers. Self help groups, therapy groups, seminars and
more are offered on-line. Professional training and
counseling are offered, also.

Other books by LuAnn Pierce available from Bohemian
Publication

Kelley . . . Longing for Home $9.95
Kelley the cat talks about her adoption and the feelings
related to her transition into her new home. Includes space
for children/youth to write or draw and questions for
parent, caregiver or therapist to discuss with the child.
Also has a place to write thoughts or notes about the
discussion. 80 pages, full color. Publication date:
March, 1997.

Chelsea's Story: Beating the Odds $12.95
Chelsea, a big black dog, tells her story about becoming
paralyzed after an accident and the struggles and triumphs
of learning to walk again. Also has space for child/youth to
write or draw and questions for adults to discuss with a
place for notes or thoughts/feelings about the discussion.
80 pages, full color. Publication date: March, 1997

Owner's Manual for Kids of All Ages: Insights on Birth
Order $21.95
One-liners in ABC format about how birth order affects
personality development. A must for siblings! Sections for
oldest, middle and youngest children. 90 pages
Publication date: January, 1997

Out of Balance: Families Under Excessive Stress $12.95
Identifies normal family transitions that can create
excessive stress and ways to successfully get through them
without malfunctioning as a family unit. Examples of
normal transitions included are birth of a child, young adult
leaving home, caring for aging parents, etc.
80 pages Publication date: November, 1996

Mending Damaged Relationship: Paths to Healing $9.95
A workbook of activities and insights about preserving
relationships. Great for families, lovers, partners, co-
workers or parent-child relationships. Step by step
instructions are included for each exercise. Normally used
by counselors for homework assignments, but designed to
be used with or without professional assistance. 64 pages
Publication date: November, 1996

Beyond the Basics: Interpersonal Skills Handbooks $10.95
each/Set of 7 $59.95
Group Counselor's Guide $49.95 each .
Handbooks on the following topics: Communication,
Problem Solving, Controlling Your Feelings, Coping with
Change and Loss, Time Management, Defining Your
Values and Beliefs, Forming and Maintaining Positive
Relationships. May be used with or without professional
assistance. Handbooks 15-25 pages each Counselor's
Guide 36 pages Publication date: November, 1996

Ordering Information

To place an order for any of these books or request updated information about other books available from Bohemian Publications write, call, fax or e-mail the following:

Name   _____

Address   _____

            _____

Phone   _____

Check all that apply:

Qty	Title
___	Kelley...Longing for Home . . . $9.95
___	Chelsea's Story: Beating the Odds . . . $12.95
___	Owner's Manual for Kids of All Ages/Insights on Birth Order . . . $21.95
___	Out of Balance: Families Under Excessive Stress . . . $12.95
___	Mending Relationships . . . $9.95
___	Beyond the Basics . . . $10.95 each
	Set of 7 handbooks . . . $59.95
___ Communications ___ Problem Solving	
___ Time Management___ Controlling Feelings	
___ Coping with Change and Loss	
___ Values and Beliefs ___ Maintaining Relationships	
___	Counselor's Guide . . . $49.95
___	Send More Information

Sub Total   ____

Shipping/Handling   5.00

Tax (TN only, .0875%)   ____

Total   ____

Bohemian Publications
PO Box 5000
Jackson, TN 38305
1-888-804-0826 PIN # 8397
e-mail: bohemian@affinitybooks.com
www.affinitybooks.com

Ordering Information

To place an order for any of these books or request updated
information about other books available from Bohemian
Publications write, call, fax or e-mail the following:

Name   _____

Address   _____

               _____

Phone   _____

Check all that apply:

Qty	Title
___	Kelley...Longing for Home . . . $9.95
___	Chelsea's Story: Beating the Odds . . . $12.95
___	Owner's Manual for Kids of All Ages/Insights on Birth Order . . . $21.95
___	Out of Balance: Families Under Excessive Stress . . . $12.95
___	Mending Relationships . . . $9.95
___	Beyond the Basics . . . $10.95 each

Set of 7 handbooks . . . $59.95

___ Communications ___ Problem Solving
___ Time Management___ Controlling Feelings
___ Coping with Change and Loss
___ Values and Beliefs ___ Maintaining Relationships
___ Counselor's Guide . . . $49.95
___ Send More Information

Sub Total
Shipping/Handling   5.00
Tax (TN only, .0875%)   _____
Total   _____

Bohemian Publications
PO Box 5000
Jackson, TN 38305
1-888-804-0826 PIN # 8397
e-mail: bohemian@affinitybooks.com
www.affinitybooks.com

Ordering Information
To place an order for any of these books or request updated information about other books available from Bohemian Publications write, call, fax or e-mail the following:

Name _____

Address _____

_____

Phone _____

Check all that apply:

Qty	Title
___	Kelley...Longing for Home . . . $9.95
___	Chelsea's Story: Beating the Odds . . . $12.95
___	Owner's Manual for Kids of All Ages/Insights on Birth Order . . . $21.95
___	Out of Balance: Families Under Excessive Stress . . . $12.95
___	Mending Relationships . . . $9.95
___	Beyond the Basics . . . $10.95 each
	Set of 7 handbooks . . . $59.95
___	Communications ___ Problem Solving
___	Time Management ___ Controlling Feelings
___	Coping with Change and Loss
___	Values and Beliefs ___ Maintaining Relationships
___	Counselor's Guide . . . $49.95
___	Send More Information

Sub Total _____

Shipping/Handling 5.00

Tax (TN only, .0875%) _____

Total _____

Bohemian Publications
PO Box 5000
Jackson, TN 38305
1-888-804-0826 PIN # 8397
e-mail: bohemian@affinitybooks.com
www.affinitybooks.com